The Way of Energy Alchemy

How To Wield Your Divine Sovereign Power for Optimal Wellbeing and Success

Unlock Your Pure Potential, Jump Timelines, And Uplevel Your Mastery of Manifestation

NATASHA SOL

Forward by Dr. Chris Chlebowski

ISBN 979-8-218-46547-6

N A T A S H A   S O L

349 East Main Street
Ashland, OR 97520

natashasol.com

For those seeking a better way,

this is for you.

You can have, be, or do anything.

This is the way.

Author's Note

"You will know the truth by the way it feels." - Unknown

Dearest Reader,

When I first began considering the idea of writing a book, I sought guidance from published authors. There was a common thread of advice among them.

Allow the process.

At the time, I was pretty certain I knew what that meant. But little did I know that part of the process would be checking my ego at the door.

I am going to be fully transparent with you here. You see, when I began this book-writing endeavor it came with a motive. To increase my reader-to-client conversion rate.

But then my shadow was illuminated to me in a big, humbling way. I received a profound lesson in authenticity and grace. And a striking reminder that there is a greater, benevolent Force at work.

So, my intention for this book shifted. It is my intention and hope that this book is a source of joyful illumination and empowerment for you. So that you may use the information presented here to cultivate optimal alignment with your highest timeline and expansion. In the highest, best, kindest, quickest, and most graceful way. I am thankful for this opportunity to be of service. If you choose to read only a few pages of this book, please skip to Chapter Three. Because it is there that you will find the illuminating truth of who you are.

Many blessings on your process.
N.S.

Natasha Sol @natashasolshine · 25 Mar

We do not receive
what we think need,
we receive what we
are ready for.

NATASHA SOL

CONTENTS

KNOW HOW TO GET YOUR BONUS MATERIAL

This is the way…

In **Chapter 4: Know How To Get What You Want - Jumping Timelines,** the Vibrational Scale helps gauge where you are. View this diagram at: **https://natashasol.com/blog/emotional-guidance-scale**.

In **Chapter 5: Know How Universal Laws Work For You - The Conscious G.E.N.I.U.S. System** is where I mention the Master's Method Of Increase. You may read more about this method at: **https://natashasol.com/access-to-the-method**.

FORWARD
by Dr. Chris Chlebowski

At this point in our species' history denying that consciousness is primarily an energetic phenomenon is a dangerously outdated perspective. Countless examples abound of the proof of this concept including near death experiences, out of place artifacts, remote viewing, the observer effect, children's recollections of past lives with irrefutable evidence, plant medicine journeys, and particle/wave behavior to name a notable few. As the bumper sticker says, "We are energetic beings having a physical experience". And as we move into the next epoch of human evolution this should be at the forefront of our minds because it has direct bearing on all fields of human science, including exploration (internal and external), physics, governance, industry, medicine, and communication.

Anyone who still doubts this perspective should note the following examples. One, it is well documented that the human heart has a measurable toric field which extends a considerable distance beyond the human body. Two, Kilian photography can objectively document a portion of the subtle energetic fields of living organisms. Lastly, millions and perhaps even billions of dollars have been spent by world governments on the study and application of telepathy and remote viewing, revealing their sincere interest in an energetic perspective. And if this is not enough evidence, persistent naysayers need only be reminded of the limited range of the human visual capability (0.0035%) out of the known electromagnetic spectrum. It seems that most of the human experience is currently unobserved.

If we are primarily energetic beings, then it is no great leap to assume that at least some part of our health and wellness is determined by the state of our energetic "body". Well-known psychics such as Dolores Cannon, Louise Hay, and Edgar Cayce as well as systems like German New Medicine all claim that most, if not all, disease originates in the nonphysical and manifests in the third dimension as "dis-ease". Many current systems of medicine utilize the non-3D locality of disease in diagnosis and treatment; acupuncture, iridology, reiki, network chiropractic, and quantum touch all routinely cure disease and yet our current methods of scientific measurement cannot yet explain their physics. Therefore, healing techniques that access the energetic aspect of our beings are likely to become the future of medicine - surpassing the current outmoded "Newtonian/mechanistic/reductionist/pharmaceuticals/disease paradigm". Quantum biofeedback, flower essence therapy, homeopathy and the like, will provide the very foundation of the next matrix of medicine. These systems will be complimented by customized nutrition, herbal medicines, physical therapies, and the very infrequent surgical or drug treatment. Those who embrace this shift will make the great leap forward in health and healing and lead the rest of the human race to a healthier and more balanced future.

The year 2019 marked the beginning of the end of the old era; the COVID-19 drama was the flash point of a great uncovering. Subsequently, old systems have rapidly deteriorated, and out of the old rises the new. Through this time, great thought leaders and new ideas have emerged. In this exciting next phase, we will need guides, signposts, and books to help us traverse the expanse; but we must choose wisely. Those who have explored across multiple disciplines and those who have Humanity's wellness as their "prioritas unum" should be ones we trust. People who have done the hard work to sort through what is true and what is not; People like Charles Eisenstein, Brett Weinstein, Teal Swan and Natasha Sol.

I see this book as one of the many that will lay the blueprint for the next matrix of healing and exploration for the human race. A book that will end up in the great arcana of health and healing of the seemingly fragile, and yet unbreakable, human race.

Let this book be a guide, but even more importantly, let it remind you that your inner knowing is your greatest ally.

Dr. John Christopher Chlebowski - May 2024

PREFACE

"The world is on fire."

A thin, frail woman stood across from me, her sunken eyes filled with tears.

Jan had been battling cancer for well over a year.

"Eight of my friends, including a past lover very dear to my heart, all died in the same year."

She lifted her fragile hand to the center of her chest as if to soothe the ache in her heart.

Underneath the sadness, I could see a faint glimmer of hope hidden in her eyes.

Feeling her gravity, I took a deep breath. "Well, I can't treat the cancer, but what I can do is support your wellness. We can soothe your pain, find your joy, and rebuild your inner strength."

She let out a long sigh of relief and the glimmer in her eyes grew brighter.

That is why I am writing this book. To fan the spark of hope to those like Jan who feel lost in…

A WORLD ON FIRE

The world is in a state of chaos we've never seen before in the history of humankind. World War is a looming threat. Extreme weather patterns that destroy life and property are frequent. New cancer cases are projected to exceed two million in 2024.[1] AI singularity is speeding towards us.[2] Open contact is imminent. Civilization, as we have known it, is collapsing. Humanity's future appears apocalyptic. And people are seeking a way through the peril and suffering.

For centuries, humans have been fixated on their physical experience of the world. The materialistic nature of our existence has been at the forefront of our focus. But now more than ever, we humans need to change our perspective and apply ourselves differently. Otherwise, the chaos will continue to consume us like wildfire.

But how? you may be asking.

Through the untapped resource of Energy Alchemy.

A new form of human consciousness is evolving out of the chaos. This expanding consciousness is awakening a power that lies within each of us. We possess the power to shift our focus towards a better future. If we choose to acknowledge and apply this power, someday in the not-too-distant future,

---

[1] Siegel, Rebecca L., Giaquinto, Angela N., Jemal, Ahmedin, "CA: A Cancer Journal For Clinicians - Cancer Statistics, 2024, (January 2024): https://doi.org/10.3322/caac.21820

[2] Musk, Elon, "AI will probably be smarter than any single human next year. By 2029, AI is probably smarter than all humans combined." (March 2024): https://twitter.com/elonmusk/status/1767738797276451090?t=dvSQsNZ9Jv1Tv759fZa-PQ&s=19

our physical bodies will have less density. And we will maneuver our world, and the galaxy, in a different way. A more harmonious way.

To get there, we must adopt a new way of being human. A more syntropic way. The new human is going to emerge one way or another. Either through a natural form of conscious evolution as described above or with nanotechnology implanted into our brains. (That will leave us subservient to controllers and void of empathy, I might add.) Those of us who prefer to experience the former rather than the latter must shake off our limitations - belief systems and programs that keep us fearful, powerless, and locked in the chaos.

We can reclaim our inner authority and rise above the flames. So that we can create and maintain a better way of life on planet Earth.

What have we got to lose? Everything.

What do we have to gain? A better way of being human. An optimal way of caring for ourselves, each other, and our home planet.

This book presents the way.

So if you are seeking a better way - a better way to live, to manifest your needs, to increase prosperity, peace, and wellbeing for all in the world - meet me in the next chapter.

INTRODUCTION:
A Catalyst For Your Expansion

"The whole point of the physical experience is the expansion beyond that Which Is."
- Abraham-Hicks

Is there a part of your life that isn't going the way you want it to?

Do you feel stuck on a health issue? A relationship? Finances? Career? Life purpose?

Consider this book a way through the stuckness. A catalyst for your expansion. A text that guides you into the most optimal version of your Self - mind, body, and spirit.

The words, phrases, and images contained within this book carry frequencies - to assist you in understanding your Divine Sovereign power and life potential. And as you receive these frequencies, energy shifts occur within you, so that you can become unstuck and activate your highest timeline. You may take this information into your dream space where your subconscious will implement the information you've received.

Trust this integration process. Because it indicates that you are awakening to a deeper understanding and conscious awareness of yourself. If you feel resistant about information presented here, pay attention. The feeling of resistance is an indication of fear-based beliefs that do not serve your highest benefit. Resistance is a sign of an unacknowledged need for healing. And without healing, fear will keep you stuck.

Nonetheless, allow yourself a natural process of assimilation. Glean and practice what resonates with devotion so that you can open and rise to your highest potential. All that you have to lose is the stuckness that is holding you back. You *can* be, do, and have what you want.

Are you ready?
Let's go.

1

KNOW WHAT YOU WANT
(A Relationship Story)

"Every time you are tempted to react in the same old way, ask if you want to be a prisoner of the past or a pioneer of the future." - Deepak Chopra

"I need clarity."

A young woman sat in a chair across from me, wringing her hands, and her eyes brimming with tears.

She hunched forward in the chair and shuffled her feet together - one foot on top of the other.

"I thought that if I talked to her, I could come clean and we could make our relationship better. But instead, things between us are worse than ever before and I'm not sure we can recover. I just don't know what to do."

The Therapy of Clarity

In every session I have with a client, I begin with the question, "What is your intention for today?" Ninety-nine percent of the time, they say they want *clarity*. They either feel lost or they are facing a tough situation and are unsure what to do about it. They need to feel clear about what they want and/or how to alleviate their pain, stress, and suffering.

To explain what I mean, let's go back to the scenario...

Emily[3] was in quite a relationship pickle. She had had an affair with her best friend. But she wasn't quite sure why she had done it. She deeply loved her wife, Jacki, for over seven years. When Emily fessed-up about the affair, Jacki, of course was heartbroken. And the trust between them was damaged. Emily was overwhelmed with remorse and worry.

After working with Emily's energy field, it became apparent to me that Emily was a people-pleaser. People-pleasing was a coping mechanism she had learned during childhood - to validate her worthiness to be loved and accepted so that she wouldn't be shamed by an overly critical mother. And in order for Emily to feel worthy to be loved by her wife - through pleasing her - she had adopted the idea of Jacki's dream life as her own.

Jacki loved living in the small, forested town where their house was located in the Pacific Northwest. She had put a lot of

---

[3] All names and personal details have been changed to honor and protect the individuals' privacy.

loving energy into their home and her place of work. But after some digging, Emily revealed to me that she longed to live near the ocean. Upon further examination, it came out that Emily was still traumatized by a wildfire that had burned their previous home to the ground. The personal unfulfillment and unaddressed trauma was a burden on Emily. She was depressed and uncomfortable about her weight. And she spent most of her time alone at home. She just wasn't sure why.

Emily wasn't aware that, based on her childhood conditioning, she feared being rejected by the person she loved the most. She didn't know that she really *needed* to be authentic about her feelings, even if it triggered those who she loved. She didn't know that she *needed* to feel safe and supported when she was being honest about *her* dreams and desires. All of these unknown reasons are what compelled Emily to have an affair. She unintentionally created a way out of the unacknowledged misery of her unfulfilled needs. Energetically, it was clear that Emily was ready to heal her childhood trauma as well as the relationships with both herself and Jacki.

Towards the end of the session, I asked Emily to tell me what she *wanted* based on the information we had uncovered.

Pondering the question for a moment, she sat straight up in her chair. "I want to feel safe to ask for what I want and need. I want to live in a place where me and Jacki *both* can be healthy and happy. And I want to feel loved for who I am, not for what I agree to do."

BOOM. Clarity. And with clarity comes release, relief, and resolution.

At this point, you might be saying…

Yeah but, Natasha, I know what I want.

Do you? Or is it just an idea that you've adopted to feel safe, loved, and accepted?

Most people *think* they know what they want. But underneath, more than they are willing to admit even to themselves, they really aren't certain. That's why 50% of new businesses fail before their fifth year in business.[4] Why the average length of a relationship is less than two years.[5] And why "only 9% of Americans that make (New Year's) resolutions complete them".[6] What people *think* they want is often an idea that's been sold to them - in the form of a belief system - by their parents, peers, spouses, social media, government, and so on. Generation after generation, the status quo has influenced us with loud, compelling voices telling us what we want without really asking us.

---

[4] Zhous, Luisa, "Small Business Statistics: The Ultimate List in 2024," (May 2024): https://www.luisazhou.com/blog/small-business-statistics/
[5] Lindner, Jannik, "Statistics About The Average Length Of Relationship," (May 2024): https://gitnux.org/average-length-of-relationship/#:~:text=Conclusion,lasting%20longer%20than%20married%20couples.
[6] Batts, Richard, "Why Most New Year's Resolutions Fail," (February 2023): https://fisher.osu.edu/blogs/leadreadtoday/why-most-new-years-resolutions-fail

It's also why so many Millennials and Gen Zs feel delusional about the American dream. It has become an impossible dream for them. This dream turned nightmare has cost them a college education with a hefty burden of debt. It gives them stress, anxiety, and sleepless nights over a job they hate. And it taunts them with the façade of a home or a lifestyle they can't afford while they work 40+ hours per week to pay for rent and bare necessities. It leaves them with feelings of hopelessness, loss, and uncertainty. Like Emily.

In order to really *know* what you want, you've gotta *feel* it.

It's a feeling of *Yeah, I'm going to be/do/have this thing.* It's not an idea, a belief, or a perspective given to you by an influential source outside of yourself.

Knowing what you want feels factual. If what you think you want falls flat in the feeling department, it's not something that you really want - it's an idea that you have adopted or idealized. This is where fantasy comes into play. And wishful thinking is where most people get lost in the maze of manifestation.

(I'll discuss "magical thinking" versus conscious creation in Chapter Two.)

Maybe you do know what you want. You're clear. You *feel* it. But you don't have all the details or know how to get there. Or you feel stuck. Or when you think about making it happen, you feel doubtful. Overwhelmed. Or afraid of losing someone you love, like Emily.

So what do you do when you are lost, stuck, doubtful, overwhelmed, or afraid?

You go within.
Groan.

I know, I know - that sounds so new agey cliché. But stick with me...

At the end of our session, I explained to Emily that there is a power within her that was waiting for her to tap into. For her to focus on. For her to expand into her *knowing*. All she needed to do is align her clarity of what she wanted with the *feeling* of having it in the present moment and act accordingly. She needed to do what she knew and *felt* was true.

The same goes for you.

Are you clear about what you want? Can you *feel* it? Does it feel *true* for you?

If not, I am happy to help guide you. Here, now, in this book. With a system that I have created and use in my own life path. This system has helped me raise three kids on my own, advance my professional career, pull myself out of poverty, improve my health after three Near Death Experiences, and publish this book.

How do I know this system works? Because I have helped hundreds of people - artists, students, couples, divorcees, parents and their children, law enforcement, doctors and their patients, business owners, psychics, actors, healers, and therapists - over 15 years get really clear on what they want and how to go about getting it. Helping others tap into their own inner sense of clarity and personal authority is what I do best.

"Natasha is a clear channel for information…" - Dr. Chris Chlebowski

"There is something so pure and clean in the execution of her work." - Misty S.

"I was mind-blown with the accuracy of the things that came up during our time together." - Kelly D.

"Still blown away by how accurate her information is…" - Issa T.

"Natasha is direct, clear, supportive, and loving in her work." - Judy May S.

So let me ask you… What is clarity worth to you? Is it worth a few moments of your time reading some pages that could change your life?

What's the least that could happen?

You get a clear, fresh, more insightful perspective of your life. You feel better. And heck, you might even manifest a thing or two.

But how, you ask?

By…
- Identifying what you really want in life, not an ideal someone has sold to you or convinced you to want
- Feeling a stable, pure, Sovereign power in the core of your being, not a faux projection of egoic-driven confidence
- Learning how to Quantum shift towards a favorable timeline, instead of stressing over the "shoe dropping" in your current one
- Manifesting the heck out of what you want, not obsessing over what you can't have
- Elevating your Life towards better health, better relations, and a better lifestyle, rather than staying stuck in lack and mediocrity

You are now at a crossroads. It is here that you decide which direction your life will take. I invite you to go the more empowered way - by tapping into your innate Sovereign power and wielding your own Energy Alchemy.

And if you think this is "magical thinking" newage (rhymes with sewage), the next chapter is for you.

2

DON'T DROWN IN DISBELIEF:
How To Overcome Your Fear

"Magical thinking refers to the idea that you can influence the outcome of specific events by doing something that has no bearing on the circumstances."[7]

"Your mind isn't magic. It's a moist computer you can program."[8]

"Why would you let me drown?"

(Remember in Chapter One when I said I would discuss the difference between magical thinking and conscious creation? Let's revisit that now. But first a story...)

---

[7] Raypole, Crystal, "Ta-Da! Magical Thinking Explained," (February 2020): https://www.healthline.com/health/magical-thinking
[8] Adams, Scott. *How To Fail at Almost Everything and Still Win Big*, pg. 3.

There is a famous parable about a man who is caught in a flood surrounding his house. He is clinging to the top of his roof pleading to God for help.

"Dear God, please save me from this flood or I will drown!"

A man swimming by towing an extra life vest hears his cries and swims towards the roof. The man calls out to the man on the roof and tells him to take the life vest so that he can put it on and float to safety. The man on the roof refuses his offer.

"God will save me!", he yells to him.

The man in the water shrugs and swims away. The man on the rooftop sees the water rising up to his knees and continues with his desperate pleas for help.

"Almighty God, please save me from this flood or I will drown!" Then a man in a boat approaches. The man calls out to the man on the roof to jump into the boat so that he can take him safely to dry land. The man on the roof shakes his head no.

"The Lord God Almighty will save me!", he yells back.

The man in the boat shrugs and paddles away. The man on the roof sees the rising water, now up to his waist, and again, cries to God for help.

"My God Almighty, please save me or I will surely drown!"

Then a man in a helicopter flies overhead. The man calls down to the man on the roof and tells him to grab the rope dangling from the helicopter. He directs him to tie rope around his waist so that he can fly him safely to dry land. The man on the roof again refuses help.

"God will save me!", he calls back.

The helicopter pilot shrugs and flies away. Eventually, the water level rises above the man's head and he drowns.

What's my point in sharing this story?

Don't let fear keep you from living a good life.

The Flood Of False Evidence Appearing Real

The story is an excellent example of the common misapplication of the Law of Attraction. Like the man on the roof, you cannot bend physical reality with mental will using opposing forces. Fear is a destructive force, not a creative one. And this is why magical thinking doesn't work.

Most humans spend a lot of mental effort worrying about bad things that *could* happen. *"I will surely drown!"*, as the man on the roof kept repeating over and over. Worrying about "what if", aka "the other shoe dropping", aligns your current timeline with a manifestation of the scenario of which you are fearful. Therefore, whatever you perceive in your reality (like the danger of drowning in a flood) is influential to your experience. Hence the phrase, "as above (in your thoughts), so below" (in your reality).

Allow me to elaborate with a visual.

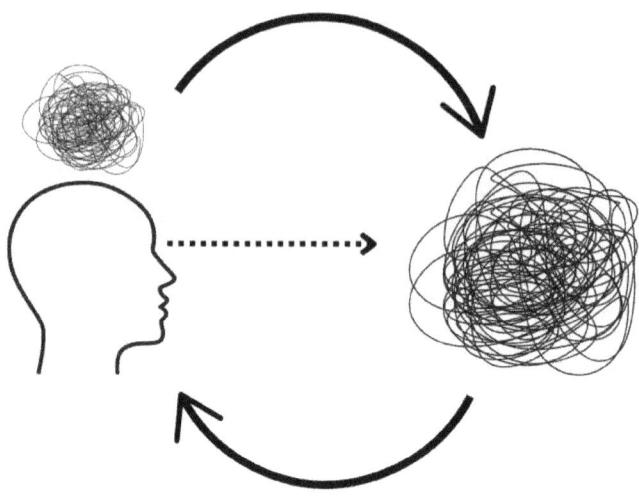

Figure 1: Cause-Reaction Feedback Loop

This is how most of us have been conditioned to react to our environment. I call it the Cause-Reaction Feedback Loop. You perceive a situation, and react to it. Your reaction perpetuates the situation and you react again. This creates an energetical rut in the mental body where your energy circles a timeline that gains no traction. The players and elements may change within the timeline, but until you respond in a different way, you will continue to have the same experience in the feedback loop. Your very own Groundhog Day.

A famous patent clerk turned professor of theoretical physics once said, "Insanity is doing the same thing over and over again and expecting different results."[9]

So in order to receive something different, you must *perceive* something different. You must shift your focus away from what you fear and into harmony with what you want. This is how we separate fantasy from conscious creation. Magical thinking tries to manipulate reality with mental will while in vibrational misalignment. Whereas conscious creation is harmonious alignment with both knowing and having through vibration created by *feelings*.

Here's a breakdown on how to do it.

1. Identify what you fear.[10]

   What is the worst-case scenario that you fear might happen? Don't try to tackle anything big or solve world events right now. Start small. For example, *I'm afraid I won't be able to pay my rent/credit card bill/car payment on time.*

   Feel your fear as you play out the worst-case scenario in your mind's eye all the way to the end. Allow yourself to feel it fully. Cry, scream, and wail if you need to. The lifespan of an emotion lasts for about 90 seconds. So I promise that you will not feel the fear forever. Breathe

---

[9] - Albert Einstein

[10] This is an important and often overlooked first step in conscious creation. Because unaddressed and untransmuted fear thwarts attempts to align your vibration with another timeline.

deeply through it as you observe the feeling move through your body. The key to your success through fear is to **fully** *feel* it.

2. After 90 seconds, ask yourself the following questions:

How likely is this worst-case scenario to happen in reality?

Not very likely. That's why it's called **F**alse-**E**vidence-**A**ppearing-**R**eal.

Can I survive if it does happen?

Probably. And you'll be stronger because of it. Not to mention wiser.

This is how to alchemize the energy of fear. Continue to pay attention to the subtle shifts that you feel in your body. The feeling of fear should wane as you observe it.

3. Once you've dissolved your feelings of fear, sorrow, and grief around the worst-case scenario, turn your attention to the next best thing that you could do. What other options besides the worst-case scenario do you have? Which feels most doable from where you are right now?

It is here that you can apply the tool of visualization. Visualization is a meditative technique that can be used to align your energy vibration with the frequency of a particular outcome. (We'll go over vibration and frequency more in Chapter Four.)

4. The final step is to do it! Commit to *do* the next best solution. Take action with the awareness that the worst-case scenario is unlikely to happen whereas the next best-case scenario is most likely to occur. Because you are putting forward-motion, creative energy into it.

How will I know it's working?

Remember Chapter One? In order to know if the system is working, you gotta *feel* it.

A creative solution *feels* true. It's clear and unclouded by unpleasant scenarios of What ifs. And through the action-oriented application of your solution, the scenario becomes resolved. A Win-Win occurs. Otherwise, if you aren't seeing positive results from your solution-based action, it's because you are still caught in the feedback loop. In order to pull yourself out of the loop, regroup your focus and energy on the next best solution. This may require digging a little deeper to identify an unacknowledged fear. It could indicate an unresolved trauma and a need for assistance from someone who can help you move through the fear objectively.

Leave F.E.A.R. Behind and Level Up

At the end of the story, the man meets God in Heaven. He inquires why God didn't save him from the flood. God answers, "I sent a life vest, a boat, and a helicopter for goodness' sake! What more did you need?"

So, the bad news is that no one, including God, is coming to *save* you. But the good news is you ALWAYS have the power you need in order to receive a solution! It's just a matter of whether you perceive that power or not. (I'll cover this more in Chapter Three.)

The man on the roof had all that he needed to get out of his worst-case scenario. He was given the next best, doable solution to his predicament - a life vest. And the next - a boat. And the next - a helicopter! But he couldn't perceive the solutions because he was circling the Cause-Reaction Feedback Loop of F.E.A.R.

You found this book for a reason. Because you are seeking a way off your own roof top. Whether it's a health issue, a toxic relationship, or money problems, something gave you an affirmative nudge to pick up or click on this book. However it came to you, you've received a way to help you get what you want. Are you going to use it or refuse it?

Don't let disbelief cause you to circle the loop. Take this book as your next best, doable solution so that you can receive what the Universe has for you - a happy, healthy, and prosperous life.

Every Conscious Creator knows the way out of a worst-case scenario is...

- To *feel* it!
- To acknowledge and fully feel fear.
- To alchemize the False-Evidence-Appearing-Real by allowing the energy to run its emotional 90-second course until it's complete.
- To identify the next best, doable scenario.
- To act on it with positive resolution!

Now that you know how to pull yourself out of the Cause-Reaction Feedback Loop, let's move on to the next chapter where I will go over how you can take your conscious creation skills to the next level. Ready? Let's go.

NATASHA SOL

3

KNOW WHO YOU ARE:
How To Tap Into Your Pure Power

"It takes a touch of genius - and a lot of courage - to move in the opposite direction." - Albert Einstein

We are sick. And not in a cool, dope, or epic way.

So many of us are infected by mediocrity. The illusion of modern life has us dazed and confused. We've become comatose by dopamine hits and unsatiated by superficial symbols of importance. And escapism is the drug of choice.

How do I know?

Consider these statistics:

- "Prescription drug use in the United States has reached record levels, rising to 6.3 billion prescriptions —

approximately 19 prescriptions for every American - filled in 2020 alone."[11]

- "About 60 million people use opioids."[12]
- Opioid overdose deaths are skyrocketing. From a steady statistic of 21,000 from 2010 to 2019 to over 80,000 in 2021. Fentanyl carries over 88% of the weight of this statistic.[13]

Everyone knows someone who is taking a prescription drug. It's become the norm. You probably also know of someone who has passed or nearly died from an overdose or drug-induced suicide. No judgment nor shame here. Life can feel unbearable at times and everyone is doing their best. My point is that this indicates an unaddressed illness that pharmaceutical drugs cannot fix. It's a greater pandemic than we ever fathomed. A *spiritual* pandemic. And the symptoms are:

- Disconnection and disillusionment
- Anxiety and detachment
- Sadness and depression
- Anger, rage, and violence
- Dis-ease - mainly cancer and heart disease

---

[11] Ho, Jessica Y., "Life Course Patterns of Prescription Drug Use in the United States," (October 2023): https://read.dukeupress.edu/demography/article/60/5/1549/382305/Life-Course-Patterns-of-Prescription-Drug-Use-in

[12] World Health Organization, "Opioid Overdose," (August 2023): https://www.who.int/news-room/fact-sheets/detail/opioid-overdose#:~:text=Among%20them%2C%20about%2060%20million,usin g%20prescription%20opioids%20is%20growing

[13] The National Institute on Drug Abuse, "Drug Overdose Death Rates," (May 2024): https://nida.nih.gov/research-topics/trends-statistics/overdose-death-rates

What is the cause of this spiritual pandemic?

We have been distracted from what is true: the larger part of ourselves. And without this awareness, it has left us open and vulnerable. We are being drained through narratives of fear, dissension, and unrest. It is clear that the siphoning off of our Life Force is causing an onslaught of mental, emotional, and physical dis-ease in our world. And it's a huge contributing factor fueling the wildfire of chaos.

In order for us to move away from this spiritual pandemic and reclaim our wellbeing, we must understand and apply ourselves differently. A perspective that can be used as a remedy to soothe the burn.

Are you ready? Here it is…

Humans are energy.

That's right.

You are more than just physical.

On a microcosm level, the space between the molecules that make up your physical structure is mostly energy. Not matter. Your biological structure is held together with energy.

YOU ARE ENERGY.

Yeah, yeah, yeah - OK, I'm energy - so what.

Before you toss this out as new age nonsense, please hear me out.

Stop for a minute.

Be still.

Open up your palms and place them lightly onto your lap.

Now breathe.

Take a deep breath and let your belly expand with your inhale.

Then gently release your breath through your mouth like you're fogging up a window.

Good.

Now two more.

Inhale deeply through your nose. Relax your jaw and exhale, through your mouth.

One more time.

In.
Out.

Now let your breath settle to its natural flow.

And listen.

Not with your ears, but with your awareness.

As you breathe with awareness, feel the flow of energy in your body.

It's subtle, below the surface, but it's there.

That's Life Force.

It's there moving through your body facilitated by your breath.

Take this moment to acknowledge this Holy Force of Life flowing within you. It's what keeps you alive!

You've just tapped into your purest source power. Nothing can come between you and this Divine Source unless you allow it to.

Breathe in this awareness.

Now expand your awareness to your present surroundings. See if you can feel Life Force moving through the things around you. A plant, a pet, another person.

Do you feel it?

EVERYTHING is energy.

Everything is created by energy, consciousness, and thought. By understanding this, physical reality takes on new meaning. People, places, and things become identifiable as forms of energy. You manipulate this energy, whether intentionally or unintentionally, consciously or unconsciously, through the energetic vibrations within your body created by your thoughts and emotions. Once you understand that your energy vibration is what facilitates your life experience, your life starts to move in a different way.

This is the way of the conscious new human, sans the brain-chip. It is the factual foundation of conscious creation and manifestation towards the life experience you want to have. It is the basis of Energy Alchemy.

What is Energy Alchemy?

Simply defined in this context, "Energy" is available power within you. And "Alchemy" is the utilization of that power to transform a focused topic into a new form, experience, or outcome.

Awareness of yourself as an Energy Being is the first, integral step to alchemizing energy. With the application of this basic understanding, you empower yourself to wield Life Force energy in ways we've only begun to imagine as the human race.

As proven in Chapter Two, Energy Alchemy is not "magical thinking". It is the application of yourself as a being who has the ability to wield powerful, creative energy in order to positively influence the world around you.

Yeah, but Natasha, why is this important? And when do we get to the part about manifesting the heck out of what I want?

In a dualistic reality, like ours, destruction is the polar opposite of creative power.

For centuries, a belief system has been passed from generation to generation based on this dualistic paradigm. A belief structure that we humans are only physical beings, separate from each other. That is just not true. It is time for us to upgrade to a new belief system based on Universal Law. We are more than just physical. And our energy is connected. We are Sovereign Beings who carry energy codes within our DNA. It's now or never for us to acknowledge this fact and activate these codes within us that will empower us as citizens of the Galactic Community. Otherwise, we will continue to succumb to the spiritual pandemic that plagues us now, destroy ourselves and our planet, and leave ourselves susceptible to brutal oppression by those who seek to control, exploit, and eradicate. Humanity has no time to lose. That's why what I am presenting here is important.

As for manifesting the heck outta stuff…

In the next chapter, I break down the application of yourself as an Energy Being in a step-by-step format so that you can jump timelines to have what you want. This system is how you learn to wield your Energy Alchemy.

As an Energy Being, you know that...

- YOU ARE ENERGY!
- EVERYTHING is created through energy, consciousness, and thought.
- You are innately Sovereign by Divine design.
- You have the inner power to create form out of the formless, and heal from the plague of destruction and dis-ease.
- The key to successful, creative manifestation is practicing the mindful awareness of these facts.

Got it? Great! Ready for the next chapter? OK, let's go!

4

KNOW HOW TO GET WHAT YOU WANT
(A Career Story)

"Human beings are also vibrating, and each individual vibrates at a unique frequency. Each one of us has the sensory skills necessary to feel the vibrations of others."
- Dr. Masaru Emoto, The Hidden Messages in Water

"What do you fear most?"

A slender, young woman with dark, captivating eyes jolted in her chair, looking surprised.

My question had struck a chord in her.

Twisting her body in the chair, the truth spilled out of her with a tearful exhale.

"I'm afraid that I'm too old."

Simone[14] had been working over a decade throughout her young adult life to make it as a recording artist and music entertainer.

"When I go to auditions in L.A., I see young, beautiful girls there, 18 or 19 years old. I think that I don't even have a chance. I'm afraid that my time has passed. And that I may never become what I've always dreamed of."

Which symbol do you think best represents Simone's emotion? This one?

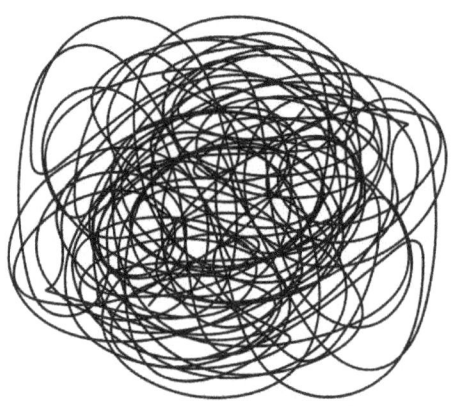

---

[14] See footnote 3.

Or this one?

If you guessed the first symbol, you are correct.

Let's time travel to that moment when Simone is twisting in the chair feeling her fear of being too old to manifest her dream career. If we took away the lovely external factors that make Simone the unique person she is and we just observed her energy, the first image is what we would see.

Let's explore this concept a little more.

When you look at the next symbol, how does it make you feel? What words would you use to describe it?

Now try the next symbol…

Feels much different from the initial one, yes?

The emotional feeling you have in your body when you are thinking specific thought forms or imagining scenarios is what

I refer to as **vibrational frequency**. Specifically in Simone's case, it was the unconscious emission of the vibrational frequency of fear. The fear of her being too old to manifest the successful career of her dreams.

What is vibrational frequency?

Frequency can be simply described as an energy signature, very similar to a bit of computer code. EVERYTHING carries a unique frequency. Even words.

For example, say the word *bitterness*. How does it make you feel?

Now try the word *satisfaction*. What shifts do you notice in your body?

One of the best studies on vibrational frequency is through the life work of Dr. Masaru Emoto, author of *The Hidden Messages in Water*. Dr. Emoto demonstrated how physical molecular formations in water could be affected by the frequencies of words, sounds, symbols, thoughts, and even intentions.

The magnetic force held within our energy frame that propels us towards the experience of a specific frequency is **vibration**. In other words, we mold physical reality with vibrational energy.

Frequency and vibration are the two main components of Energy Alchemy. You can use words and images to activate a vibration within your energy field in order to align with the frequency of a desired timeline.

On an individual level, frequency serves as a targeted destination. I like to think of it as the orange pin on a maps app. Vibration acts as the vehicle. You may drive your vehicle of vibration aimlessly, allowing the emotions of an undirected focus (with little or no intention) to dictate your next destination. This approach may seem that you have no control over your vehicle, much less where you are going.

Or a more empowered approach is to aim your vehicle of vibration with intention towards the desired destination by identifying its frequency. This is the basic premise of...

Timeline Jumping

Now you really have my attention, Natasha! How do I jump timelines?

Let me break it down for ya.

1. Assess and accept where you are.

Analyze your current situation[15] and take responsibility for it so that you can change it.

Yes, bad things happen to good people. But a victim mentality doesn't serve any benefit. Being a victim of your current

---

[15] "The Emotional Guidance Scale" is a fantastic tool in identifying where you are in vibration. You may view this diagram at: https://natashasol.com/blog/emotional-guidance-scale

circumstances doesn't help you feel better. And it certainly doesn't help you get to a better place.

You must decide that you are going to take responsibility for the outcome and direction of your life. And use your current resources to make it better. Because when you do, you empower yourself to pull out of an unfavorable loop.

2. Identify what you really want.

Now that you accept responsibility for your current situation and are keenly aware of what you don't want in your current set of circumstances, flip the coin. Doing so shifts your vibration. Consider the exact opposite of what you don't want in order to identify the timeline that you do want to experience.

This step is necessary in order to pull yourself out of the Cause-Reaction loop. Without a new timeline to focus on, you are more likely to get sucked back into the loop of what you don't want.

3. Decide you are going to shift your perspective.

You must make an affirmative decision that you are going to focus the bulk of your thoughts, time, and energy on the desired timeline that you want to experience. **EVEN IF IT IS DIFFICULT AT FIRST**. You have to *commit daily* to your new focus. And redirect your thoughts in order to *activate* the frequency of the new timeline in your energy field.

This third step moves your vibration into a frequency of **empowerment** so that you can manifest what you want. When you shift your vibe, you "jump" to the other timeline.

How do I know when I've successfully jumped timelines?
You will *feel* different! You will present yourself differently. People will respond to you differently. Different, new, and exciting people will approach you. New opportunities in alignment with the new timeline will arise. Different circumstances will unfold into your experience.

When you focus on your desired timeline, it's important that you attune your vibration of living, being, and having what you want in the present moment. Otherwise, the timeline hangs in a future mirage that never comes to fruition. Remember, you gotta *feel* it!

Attachment versus Activation

When I scanned Simone's energy field, it was apparent that she was destined for greatness. Her artistic genius was activated and her creative energy flowing. But she was *attached* to the way her desire should manifest. That is, the rote method of how entertainers become successful.

Attachment creates resistance in the field of possibility. It slows down manifestation. Attachment to a specific course will not manifest what you are wanting to receive even if you are diligent with your actions. Like Simone.

Simone created dissonance in her energy field by holding onto a specific sequence of events and situations in which she was afraid she had no chance of success. Letting go of her attachment to a specific timeline would allow her to activate her vibration to the frequency of a better, more successful outlet for her creativity. And this is what she did exactly. After our session together, Simone decided to focus on the *feeling* of being successful in her own unique way. She shifted her perspective, set an intention, and acted upon it. She used a system to attain her goals, not just magical thinking. And now, her creative genius is flowing and her career is flourishing with success because she is vibrationally aligned and taking action towards her desired timeline.

Remember the way to jump timelines is to:

1. Accept where you are
2. Identify where you want to be
3. Shift your vibe to match the desired frequency

What happens next?

In the next chapter, we learn how to meld this method together with Universal Laws so that you become an unstoppable force of Conscious GENIUS! Are you ready? Let's go!

5

KNOW HOW UNIVERSAL LAWS WORK FOR YOU
(A Healing Story)

"Positive affirmations, when they are reinforced with positive actions and practiced over a sufficient period of time, can rebalance emotional energy and help initiate healing." - Harvey Bigelsen, M.D.[16]

"UGH. I feel stuck."

The discouragement and frustration weighing on the 36-year-old woman sitting across from me was palpable.

Talia[17] had been struggling with a chronic illness for over three years. She was diligent in following her doctor's protocol but her healing seemed to be taking for-ev-ver.

"I am grateful for the progress I am making, but I'm frustrated

---

[16] Bigelsen, Harvey. *Holographic Blood: A New Dimension In Medicine,* pg. 60.
[17] See footnote 3.

that it's taking me so long to recover. I just don't know what my body needs to heal."

I hear this a lot from clients who are facing a health issue or illness. Like Talia, if you're investing your time and energy into something that doesn't seem to be resolving itself, the burden can feel excruciating. Especially when physical discomfort or pain is involved. Thought patterns can sound like…

- *I can't…*
- *I hate having to…*
- *No matter what I do…*
- *Nothing's working!*

Or like Talia said that day in my office, *UGH.*

Let's use a visual to understand what's going on energetically. Take a look at the image in Figure 2. The scribbled blotch represents a timeline with illness. The person perceives illness in their body and experiences it.

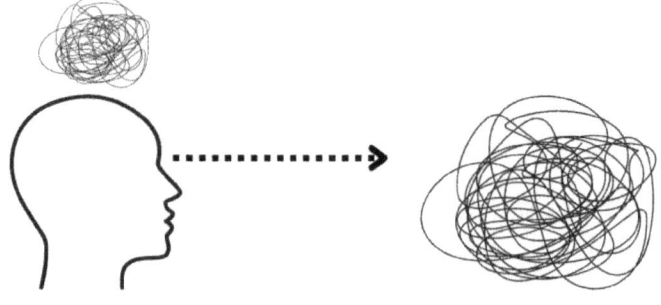

Figure 2: Perceiving the Experience

Figure 3: Attempting to Change the Experience

The person may try to change the experience, indicated by the wavy lines in Figure 3, but they still *perceive* illness in their body and hold the *vibration* of it in their energy field.

So even if the person does their very best to physically change the outcome of their illness - with changes in diet, taking medication, or even surgery - without changing their perception or vibration, the illness persists one way or another. As a result, a Cause-Reaction Feedback Loop becomes predominant in their energy field and their experience with the illness continues. This is how the feeling of stuckness is created, fueled by the vibrational energy of frustration, as shown in Figure 4.

Figure 4 is what I see energetically in a person's field who is stuck on *fixing* their illness rather than *being* well. The person in the diagram has put a lot of effort into *doing* what they think will make the illness, pain, and suffering go away rather than *embodying* good health. Can you feel the difference? In other words, the person is still focusing their energy on the problem instead of receiving and implementing the solution.

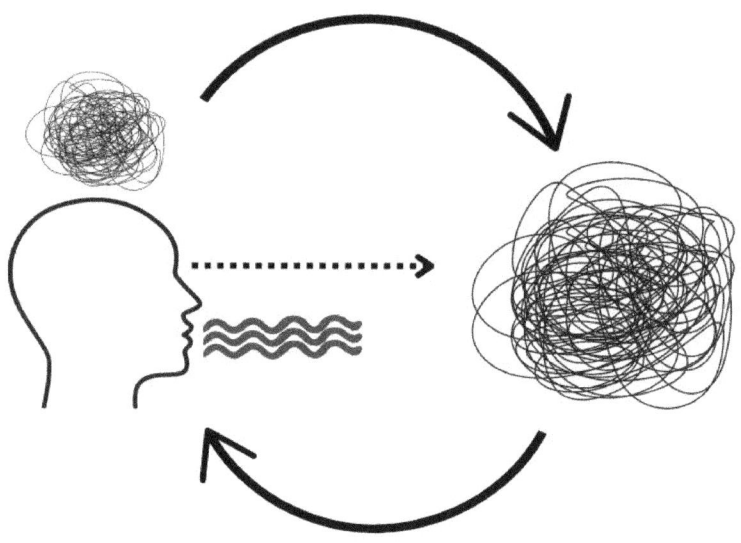

Figure 4: Cause-Reaction Feedback Loop with Attempts To Change the Experience

So how do you unstick the feedback loop and allow wellbeing? With a system.

A system? Why a system?

"People who use systems do better... A system is something you do on a regular basis that increases your odds of happiness in the long run."[18]

---

[18] Adams, Scott, *How To Fail at Almost Everything and Still Win Big*, pg. 32-33.

An applied system ensures your desired manifestation - in this case, your chances of feeling, being, and staying healthy. The system that I propose in this book can be applied to *anything* that you feel stuck, frustrated, or confused about, whether it's relationship, career/work, money/finance, or health-related issues. It's…

The Conscious G.E.N.I.U.S. System

G-auge

E-stablish

N-ail

I-nitiate

U-plevel

S-ecure

Everyone's biological make-up is unique because of our differing experiences, genetics, constitution, toxicity-load, etcetera. But this system is one that everyone can use because we have one thing in common… We all are ENERGY BEINGS!

Here's the breakdown of the G.E.N.I.U.S. system:

1. **GAUGE WHERE YOU ARE. Acknowledge and release the blocks.**

In Chapter Four, I covered how an important first step towards a new timeline is to take responsibility for your experience so that you can change it.[19] The Universal Law of Correspondence helps you do just that.

The Law of Correspondence states that what happens around us is a direct reflection of what is occurring within us. Hence the adage, "as above" - in your thoughts - "so below" - mirroring in your body and life experience. We use this law as a guide to help us take responsibility for manifested timelines and identify blocks impeding wellness.

Saying that, illness is not what blocks you from being well. Wrap your noggin around that one. In fact, there are no "blocks", just energy. "Blocks" *are* energy.

"Blocks" are beliefs and associated thought patterns. I often see beliefs in my clients' energy fields as trauma or social conditioning. (I'll discuss this more in Chapter 8.) When you experience trauma or obstructive conditioning at an early age, belief systems are formed as a survival tactic to keep you safe. These systems, executed by the subconscious, continue throughout your lifetime. A locked loop of energy recreates the same familiar experiences and outcomes over and over again. Negative self-talk is a form of a belief system. Maybe you've heard someone affirm a self-deprecating statement

---

[19] Pg. 42.

like, "I'm stupid because I always choose the wrong people to date!".

They probably have a long list of failed relationships. That is because their subconscious is a running belief system that compels them to choose accordingly. Sometimes this repeating energy loop creates an unconscious irritation, resulting in dissonance that causes a physical, mental, or emotional breakdown, leading to dis-ease. So we use the Law of Correspondence to pin-point a belief in order to release the energy that caused the illness.

Whenever I guide a client to discharge a belief system that is causing illness, they often experience a huge emotional release. And they report feeling lighter and more relaxed afterward. If you do not feel a comforting sense of relief and relaxation after applying this step, there is probably something more in your energy field that needs to be addressed and released.

Once the root cause of the illness is released, this frees up your energy field to establish a greater flow towards what you want.

2. ESTABLISH WHAT YOU WANT. Reset the field.

Now that you've disengaged the illness-causing belief system and its attached emotions, you can turn your attention towards what you want to manifest - a healthy body![20]

---

[20] I am NOT suggesting here that you should ignore necessary medical attention in order to be well. In life-threatening health challenges like

In this step, we exercise the Universal Law of Polarity. This is my favorite law out of all the laws because it assists in gaining crystal clear clarity on what is really wanted. It is the law that rules timeline jumping, which can be applied to reset your energy field towards a new timeline. You do this by examining contrasting situations or experiences, as shown in Figure 5. Which do you choose to focus your energy on? UGH as indicated by the scribbled blotch or AHHH as represented by the wavy lines?

Figure 5: Examining Contrasting Situations with The Law of Polarity

Once you've measured the contrast of your UGH versus your AHHH and you've redirected your field towards the desired timeline, you can then apply the Universal Law of Vibration.

3. NAIL THE SOLUTION. Activate the vibration.

---

cancer and heart disease, please always seek professional assistance from a trustworthy medical provider who supports your health and wellness, not sickcare. Be smart and use your discernment, follow your doctor's recommendations, and focus your mind, body, and spirit on healthy living.

Remember in Chapter Four, when I said everything is vibrating at its own signature frequency?[21] That is the premise of the Universal Law of Vibration. Your *vibration* matched with the *frequency* of your desired timeline is what kicks the Law of Attraction into action. And you become energetically magnetized to what you want. It is *vibration* in formless energy that molds physical reality!

Sensory awareness in your body is key to activating vibration. This is when the tool of visualization comes in handy. Visualization helps you nail down the vibration of the solution you want to manifest. First you identify the polar opposite of the old timeline and then visualize it.

Use visualization of the new timeline to dial your vibration to the frequency of it so that you can conjure the *feeling* of it. Remember Chapter One? You gotta *feel* it![22]

Be sure to feel it **now** in the present moment so that your experience becomes connected to it. This application of the Law of Vibration is what generates the magnetic, like-attracts-like effect that so many Law of Attraction teachers talk about.

Be aware that it is not visualization itself that connects you to your desired manifestation. This is a common misconception people make in the application of the Law of Attraction. They try to force something into manifestation by constraining themselves to think about it over and over again. Remember,

---

[21] Pg. 41.
[22] Pg. 15.

like the man on his rooftop, you can't bend physical reality with mental power. As a matter of fact, the energy of consciousness creation lies within the body, specifically in the Heart, Solar Plexus, and Sacral chakras, not in the mind as so many people think. The mind identifies the possible paths but it is vibrational energy within the body that drives the vehicle of experience towards manifestation.

In Figure 6, it is shown that even if the outer circumstances haven't shifted, as indicated by the scribbled blotch, the person has shifted their vibration through mindful focus, as indicated by the wavy lines. They perceive and *feel* the new timeline even if it hasn't begun to manifest on the physical plane, yet.

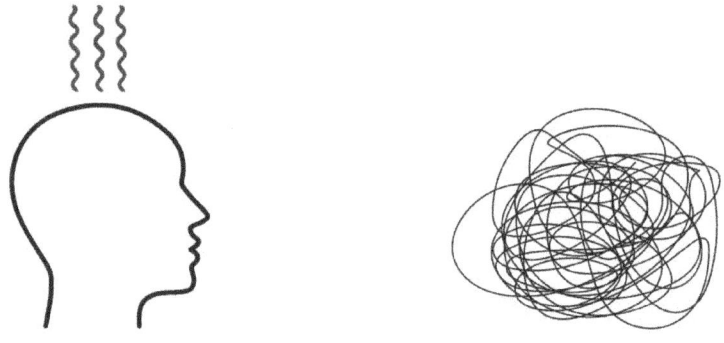

Figure 6: Activating a New Vibration

Now that you've activated the frequency of your desired timeline in your vibrational energy field, you can apply the next law.

4. INITIATE ACTION - Implement the new way.

Once you have the solution-oriented timeline activated within your energy field, apply the Universal Law of Cause and Effect. This law states that every single action produces a reaction. No matter what.

Study the sequence of diagrams in Figure 7. See that awareness has been redirected away from the illness, shown by the scribbled blotch, and towards the new timeline of well-being indicated by the wavy lines. At this point, you can begin to implement manifestation by setting a new *cause* into action.

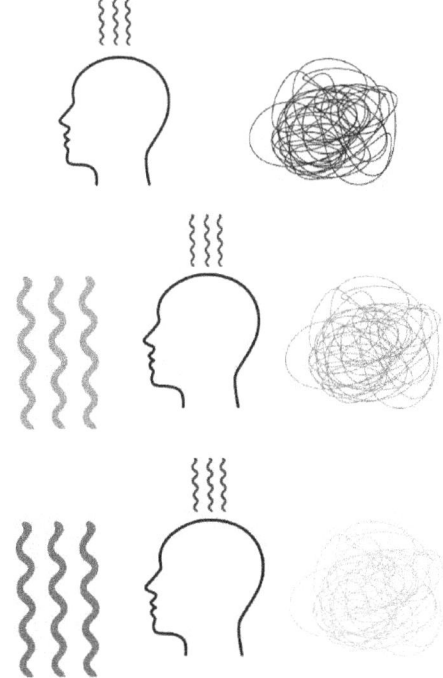

Figure 7: Shifting Away From The Old Timeline

Figure 8: The Effects of the New Timeline

As the frequency of the new timeline becomes stronger in your vibrational field, shown in Figure 8, you will see the *effects* of it become more apparent in your experience.

Meanwhile, the effects of the old timeline fades. Until finally, all that you perceive and experience is the total and complete manifestation of the new timeline.

So take action! Make your *causes* - decisions, choices, and **daily** tasks - align with the desired *effect* of the new timeline. Be willing to break out of your comfort zone otherwise, you are not going to manifest the effect you want. And seize moments of opportunity because serendipity often leads to WIN-WIN scenarios that you didn't consider before. Follow the power of your YES!

Wait a minute, all of this sounds familiar, Natasha.

Well, yeah. If you've been around the LOA block a time or two, this information is nothing new. BUT *the way* that it is presented here is evolutionary. This is an applicable *system* based on *multiple* Laws of the Universe, not just one - the Law of Attraction - that so many spiritual teachers talk about. Here you are given *all* the puzzle pieces to help you successfully manifest what you want.

This system activates the awareness of yourself as an Energy Being. And it helps you utilize the energy that exists within your biological frame, pulsing amidst your cells, flowing between your molecules, to create and manifest the life you desire to live. No neurochip required. This is the exact system we used in Chapter Two to avoid drowning in the flood of F.E.A.R. Remember the man on his roof? He could have been a G-E-N-I - oh wait, I still have two letters left to go…

5. UPLEVEL YOUR INTENTION. Use the Method of Increase.

Once you've set your intention and activated it in your energy field, use the Method of Increase to create form in the formless and bring it to fruition into your physical reality.[23] For example, talk about your intention with absolute certainty that it will manifest. Facilitate positive action to increase its energy. Introduce thought forms to others that will repeat and ripple

---

[23] See Know How To Get Your Bonus Material for more information on the Method Of Increase.

through the ethers of creation adding energy to your planted seed of intention. Give what you want to receive![24]

6. SECURE YOUR SUCCESS.

This is my favorite step of the system. And I think you'll see why. There is a vibration above all others when it comes to securing manifestation. Most would say it's love. And while yes, unconditional love is the highest frequency in the Universe, I am talking about a frequency specific to *manifestation*.

So, what's the frequency, Kenneth? It's...

The Power Of Gratitude

You see, gratitude is more than just saying thank you. It's a frequency that works like a power-up when you apply it to your Energy Alchemy.

When you are authentically grateful for the opportunity to manifest, the vibration and its natural by-vibe of humility kickstarts Universal Forces into action.

The feeling of gratitude moves you into a place that what you've asked for, *has been given*. No question. No doubt. It's done. In fact, I encourage you to spend more time *feeling grateful* for what has yet to manifest instead of spending it on

---

[24] The Universal Law of Equivalent Exchange states that anything given you must receive something with greater value and for anything received or expected you must give something of equal or greater value.

your vision board. Assume and feel grateful that your request has been heard. The order is in. On its way to the destination. Soon to be delivered. So, say thank you! And *mean* it.

Once you begin to apply the feeling of gratitude to your Energy Alchemy, you may find yourself feeling more joyful as life takes on an ease that wasn't there before.

Like Talia.

Once Talia understood that she was spending more time *fixing* her illness instead of *being* healthy, she was able to find a wellness care program that worked well for her. She redirected her focus and energy towards proactivism for her health - mind, body, and spirit. And as a result, she felt inspired and free from the dreaded, heavy feeling of being stuck.

Now that we've covered all the steps of the system, let's simplify things.

Every Conscious G.E.N.I.U.S. knows that in order to successfully master manifestation, you must...

1. Embrace responsibility for what is in your current experience and release your "blocks".
2. Turn your attention towards what you want.
3. Feel it!
4. Initiate manifestation through daily, intuitively-guided action.
5. Give what you want to receive.
6. *Feel* grateful that it's done!

OK GENIUS, now that you have the system down, are you ready to master those Alchemy skillz? Great! Let's go!

6

KNOW HOW TO HONE YOUR MASTERY OF MANIFESTATION

"Successful people don't wish for success, they decide to pursue it. And to pursue it effectively, they need a system."
- Scott Adams

Reflecting on the examples I've shared in the previous chapters, what do you think Emily, Simone, and Talia's stories have in common?

You got it - it's a system. A system of *doing* to be exact.

Most of us humans adhere to a concept that success comes from doing hard work. Just do a Google search and you'll find lots of quotes from famous people saying how hard work is what made them successful. Popular marketing adages like 'Just do it' and 'Let's do this' are other examples of how saturated our culture is with this system.

Now I'm not saying that doing hard work can't yield a successful payoff. But what if I told you that hard work equals success isn't entirely accurate? It's not the hard effort of *doing* that earns success, it is *embodying* success itself that makes one successful.

I know that might sound contradictory to what I told you in Chapter Five about taking action on a new timeline[25] but bear with me.

The reason why people succeed from hard work is because they *believe* it will. And because they believe in hard work, the actions associated with it helps them to embody success until it manifests. The *belief* of hard work equals success is a *system* that aligns vibration with the desired manifestation of success. Get it?

I'll discuss this more in Chapter Eight but for now, I wanna share with you a few simple exercises that can help you embody success and hone your mastery of manifestation.[26]

A Tip, A Trick, and A Tactic

First a tip...

A Power Affirmation

"I CAN, I WILL, I AM."

---

[25] Pg. 57

[26] But if you just can't wait to read more about the frequency of success, go to page 77.

This is one of the most powerful mantras I've practiced. It is The Equalizer to self-doubt. Even if you are feeling uncertain, afraid, or uncomfortable about something you want to accomplish, this mantra will give you a confidence lift to step out of your comfort zone and launch forward towards what you want. Say it with feeling and affirm it daily!

You can also add specifics to the mantra of what you want to manifest. For example, "I *can* be healthy. I *will* be healthy. I *am* now healthy!" Remember to say it with *feeling*!

Now a trick...

Smile Your Way To Success

There's a song by a famous jazz singer named Nat King Cole that I have loved ever since I was a child. The lyrics go like this:

Smile though your heart is aching
Smile even though it's breaking
When there are clouds in the sky
You'll get by

If you smile through your fear and sorrow
Smile and maybe tomorrow
You'll see the sun come shining through
For you

Light up your face with gladness
Hide every trace of sadness
Although a tear

May be ever so near

That's the time you must keep on trying
Smile, what's the use of crying?
You'll find that life is still worthwhile
If you'll just smile

I love this song because the sentiment is so wise and simple to do.

The trick is to smile without reason. Mindfully practice smiling *all the time* even if you are sitting alone. Because when you smile, you signal to your brain and your body that you are happy, joyful, and at ease. Smiling curbs negative self-talk too! When you smile for no reason, you naturally feel better and emit a vibration of joy, peace, and happiness to those around you. Because people like being around happy, successful people! Try it! You will be amazed at the results when you do this simple thing.

Finally, a tactic...

Programming The Subconscious

When you go to bed, ask your Higher Self to help you integrate positive feelings while you are sleeping. Generate good vibes as you fall asleep and expect to feel different in the morning. When you wake up in the morning, say "thank you for helping me feel better!". This is especially helpful when you are dealing with morning anxiety - intend the night before to feel uplifted and easeful when you wake.

You can also ask your Higher Self to help you integrate the frequency and feeling of a desired timeline that you want to manifest. For example, if you want to lose weight but you are having a difficult time imagining what it would feel like to be slimmer, ask! Imagine the feeling as you fall asleep and expect to feel different in the morning. Upon waking, say "Thank you for my slimmer body!". Then implement the feeling with your inspired action throughout the day. Just BE it!

Every Conscious Genius knows:

That success can be *embodied* through aligned action.

Yeah, but Natasha, I've tried stuff like this before and it didn't work. How can I be sure that the G.E.N.I.U.S. system and all of these tricks will work?

I'm so glad you asked! Because the next chapter is for you. Ready? Let's go.

7

THE YEAH BUTS

"There is always a way - if you're committed."
-   Tony Robbins

"I tried it. It doesn't work."

"It's too hard."

"It goes against my religious beliefs."

These quotes are examples of what I like to call the System of Not.

Here's another example:

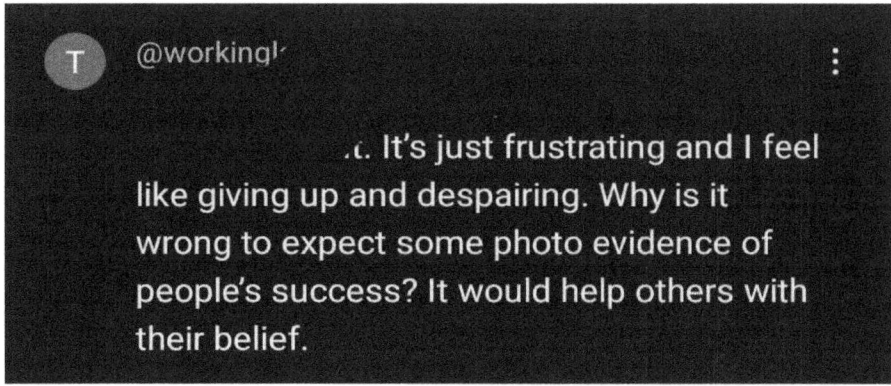

I'm going to break it to you... If you are waiting around for some kinda "proof" before you believe in your innate power to manifest, well, you're NOT going to get any because your vibration is dialed to disbelief.

Yeah, but Natasha...

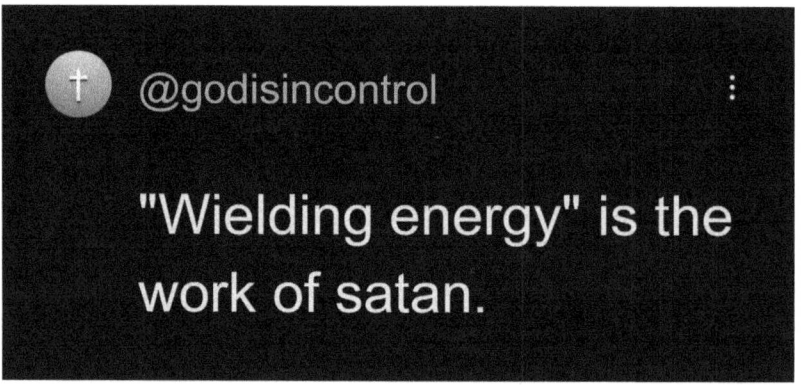

Based on the Christian premise, God is living inside of us. It is the power of God-Divine-Source-Creator that moves through us. The same power that allowed Moses to part the sea, Ezekiel to prophesy, Jonah to survive being swallowed by a whale, David to slay a giant, Daniel to close the mouths of hungry lions, Esther to save her people from being slaughtered, and Yeshua to heal the sick. You get the picture. Yeshua said, "the works that I do, you shall do also, and greater works than these shall you do".[27] This power inspires us to use all of our facilities to serve the Divine I AM ALL THAT IS to our greatest abilities. The G.E.N.I.U.S. system does not defy that. It propels it.

---

[27] Christian Bible, John 14:12

Yeah, but…

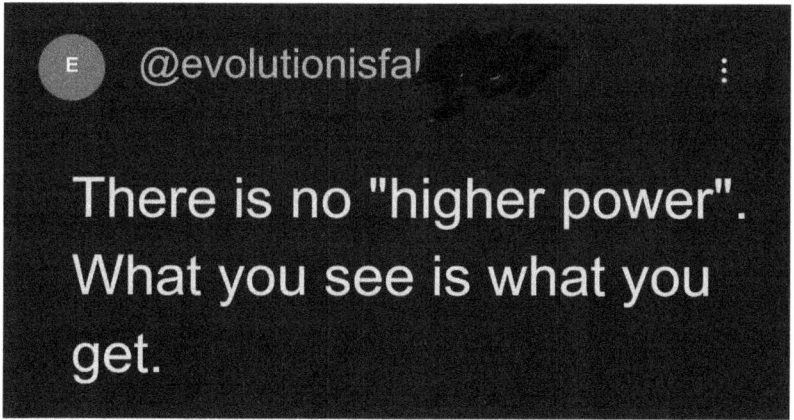

Atheism is another belief system. And you have the power of freewill to decide if that system is working for you or not.

You see, everyone one of us is running some sort of system, either consciously or unconsciously. And if you're running the program of Not, you're *not* going to manifest what you want. In fact, based on the Law of Polarity we covered in Chapter 5, you will manifest the exact opposite.

So how do you untie the Not?

You *decide* to.

Deciding versus Wanting

If you sit around wanting something while affirming it's *not* going to happen, well the Universe is NOT going to show up for you. (The Law of Correspondence, remember?) When you make a clear *decision* that you are going to have, be, or

do something that you want to achieve, you set Universal Forces into action.
Yeah, but…

I'm so glad you asked! I'm going to go off on a tangent here because I feel like it's important for you to know.

In Chapter 5, I mentioned how in order to implement the frequency of the new timeline, you *must* take action and seize moments of opportunity. This includes…

Asking For What You Want

Most people are afraid of asking for what they want. Women typically have a hard time asking for what they want or need in a professional setting. Whereas men have a difficult time asking for what they want or need in a relationship.

I once had a friendly acquaintance whom I had met in a dance class. It became very clear to me and everyone else that this man wanted to be more than "just friends". He would drop all kinds of hints that he wanted to go out with me but he would not ask me out.

Men often exude this type of behavior when it comes to relationships. A fear of rejection or being perceived as vulnerable causes them to avoid asking for what they want.

Asking for what you want doesn't make you weak or vulnerable, it empowers you! If you're not asking for what you want, it can make you look sus, creepy, or like an a-hole. When you ask for what you want in a clear, direct, and respectful approach, your energy isn't muddled with fear or manipulation. It's sexy! Women love a man (or those who lean into their masculine aspect) who knows what he wants, who isn't afraid to ask, and at the same time shows respect. If you ask with a clear intention and your request is rejected, don't take it personally! Consider it a good indication that a better opportunity more in alignment with your desires is available to you.

The same goes for women (or those who lean into their feminine aspect) in the workplace. Whenever a co-worker receives a promotion, bonus, or raise, women will notoriously moan, bicker, stonewall, manipulate, or backstab but will not *ask* for what they want!

For many years, I was the hiring manager at the clinic where I work. One time, I posted a job that stated the pay rate was $20 per hour. While interviewing the top picks, all women, I asked each one for their desired pay rate. Every candidate, except for one, requested a dollar amount that was *less* than what was offered on the job ad. Less! The one candidate who didn't request less asked for the exact amount that was listed on the job posting. I thought this was illuminating about how women perceive their worthiness to receive what they want in a professional environment.

Going back to the main point of the chapter…

In order to shift your energy from the Not system to the G.E.N.I.U.S. system, *decide* to manifest what you want and *ask* with clear intention. Because when you do, you will feel your self-worth grow and flourish. And when your self-worth is higher, you feel confident and inevitably attract success! See how that works? Good!

Every Conscious Creator knows that:

- The way to successful manifestation is to *decide* to go for it!
- Empowered achievers *always ask* for what they want!
- Masters don't "yeah, but" - they E X P A N D (like, in the next chapter).

8

E X P A N D INTO A NEW, MASTERFUL YOU

"Believe it can be done. When you believe something can be done, really believe, your mind will find the ways to do it. Believing a solution paves the way to solution."
- David J. Schwartz

When the world governments locked down the nations in 2020, everyone was forced to take a pause. No other time in the history of modern civilization did we experience the collective energy as we did during the pandemic. Since that pause, hundreds of thousands of people have awakened to a greater awareness of our connection to each other and the planet.

Humanity has entered a phase of evolution where we must work together in order to ascend in consciousness and heal the planet. We all *feel* a *knowing* that something's gotta change.

Another reason why it is time for us to expand into a different way of being human is because the frequencies of our planet are on the rise. Earth has shifted into a higher dimensional, fourth-density plane. Soon, we will no longer be able to sustain the lower frequencies of a third-dimensional world. Intense weather patterns, new planetary transits[28], and coronal mass ejections from the Sun are clear indications of this increase in frequency.

And "The Great Solar Flash" as depicted on The Great Awakening Map is expected to play a significant part.

The Great Solar Flash is a prophetic event when the sun will emit a great flash of light forcing all of humanity into a higher frequency and an evolved state of consciousness. While we can only speculate if and when this event will occur, I believe that smaller, yet powerful, events are already occurring. The sun is actively emitting unusual CMEs. In May 2024, NASA scientists observed at least seven coronal mass ejections that created an extreme, level 5 out of 5, geomagnetic storm.[29] And solar activity is expected to increase.[30]

Whether or not a big flash of light from the sun will lift us into higher states of consciousness is debatable. But we can be certain that intense planetary and solar shifts are indeed

---

[28] Markauskiene, Daiva Kristina, "2024: A Leap into the Aquarian Age?", (September 2020): https://astrodaiva.com/en/uncategorized/2024-a-leap-into-the-aquarian-age/#:~:text=Pluto%20transits%20from%20Capricorn%20into%20Aquarius&text=Along%20with%20this%20transit%2C%20humanity,21%20to%20September%202%2C%202024.

[29] Space Weather Prediction Center, National Oceanic and Atmospheric Administration, "Historic Geomagnetic Storm Continues," (May 2024): https://swpc.noaa.gov/news/historic-geomagnetic-storm-continues

[30] Fox, Nicola, "Solar Cycle 25 is Exceeding Predictions and Showing Why We Need the GDC Mission," (July 2022): https://blogs.nasa.gov/solarcycle25/2022/07/27/solar-cycle-25-is-exceeding-predictions-and-showing-why-we-need-the-gdc-mission/

occurring. And no doubt they are currently affecting the solar system, our home planet, and our state of being. How we integrate the energy is up to us.

The Necessity of Healing

If we want to survive these shifts and manifest a better, more peaceful world filled with wellbeing and abundance for all, we must face the pain of our individual suffering and allow ourselves to receive healing. Doing so guarantees the healing of Earth and steers humanity towards a better future.

Without healing, the future of life on planet Earth is bleak.

But how do we heal?

Let's revisit what I began in Chapter Six about the reality of success.

Everything is energy, right? Well, so is success. Success at its very bare bones of existence is a frequency. That's why so many life/business/success coaches refer to success as an attitude. It's not *doing* that yields manifestation of success - it's alignment with the frequency of it.

The same could be said about healing.

Healing is a Frequency

As I mentioned in Chapter Five,[31] healing isn't an action, it's a way of alignment. Healing is not about doing, fixing, or trying to force physical, mental, or emotional wellness into manifestation. It's about *embodying* the frequency of wellbeing. But in order for us to embody the frequency of wellbeing for ourselves and the world, we must face and release our trauma.

Illness is Trauma

> **"Shock, fright, terror and panic even if only once experienced, can cause chronic effects through muscle tensions unresolved."[32]**

Illness always traces back to sustained trauma. The energy of trauma is what sets a domino-effect into motion towards dis-ease that eventually surfaces in the body, mind, or spirit. It's illuminating that the entire world was shut down for a virus, isn't it?

Everyone has suffered from some sort of trauma. During childhood, we either received too much of one thing or not enough of another. Some have more severe experiences than others. But we are the same in our need for healing through the Divine Force of unconditional Love.

---

[31] Pg. 53-54.
[32] Turland, Jill R., *A Miracle A Day: Using Very High Potency Homeopathy*, pg. 1.

So if you are facing a mental, physical, or emotional health issue, it's a good bet that there is unresolved trauma in your energy field. I invite you to examine your childhood to pinpoint where the root cause of illness could have begun so that you can release the trauma and receive healing.

The Bigger Picture

To heal ourselves is both our individual and collective task. It is something that we must do before we can "save the world" because we cannot give what we haven't done for ourselves. Furthermore, it is our work to align with, adjust to, and create the higher dimensional existence of New Earth as light codes from the Sun come barreling towards us.

"How will I know I've been treated with the upgrade codes for 5th density of New Earth?"

In the words of the late, great Whitney Houston, 'how will I know'? When you activate the frequency of what you want in your vibration, including the frequencies of fifth-dimensional New Earth, you will know by your **feelings**! Can you feel it? Then you've got it!

The New Human

The new human is less about doing and more about *being*. It is you *being* the embodiment of your Soul. This requires you to *embody* the frequencies of what you want in faith and

Masterful Knowing. And then follow through with intentional action using your Energy Alchemy.[33]

Furthermore, Energy Alchemy isn't about your ego getting all the superficial stuff that you think will make you happy. It's about you *aligning* with your highest, most optimal timeline that already exists. Right here. Right now. In this moment, as you breathe with Divine Life Force.

"What exactly is your 'highest timeline'?"

Your highest timeline is the life purpose that your Soul signed up for before you incarnated into this lifetime. Humans do not incarnate to suffer. We come to learn and expand Universal consciousness. But we unconsciously choose to suffer. So when you set an intention to align with your highest timeline, you are choosing to do what your Soul agreed to do. It's what you came for after all!

Healing A World On Fire

In summary, the way to heal a chaotic world is to consciously choose to heal ourselves by releasing our trauma. It is up to each of us to reclaim and activate the pure power of our Divine Sovereignty. And in order to build a better, more peaceful, and harmonious world that we all dream of, we must intentionally align our vibration with the highest, optimal timeline. The systematic way of Energy Alchemy can empower us to successfully do that.

---

[33] "Faith without works is dead," Christian Bible, James 2:17.

It is my hope that you have gleaned at least some nuggets of information presented here to help you expand into the healthy, fulfilling, prosperous life experience you want. So be it, in the highest, best, and most optimal way. Thank you for giving me the opportunity to work with you. Now go out there and manifest like a master, Genius. (Psst, remember to check out your bonus material on the next page!)

KNOW HOW TO GET YOUR BONUS MATERIAL

This Is The Way…

In **Chapter 4: Know How To Get What You Want - Jumping Timelines,** the Vibrational Scale helps gauge where you are. View this diagram at: **https://natashasol.com/blog/emotional-guidance-scale**.

In **Chapter 5: Know How Universal Laws Work For You - The Conscious G.E.N.I.U.S. System** is where I mention the Master's Method Of Increase. You may read more about this method at: **https://natashasol.com/access-to-the-method**.

Acknowledgements

To my "Chickens", Sage, Kira, and Severin, thank you for giving me reason to never give up. I love you beyond the moon and back.

Dr. Chris and Samae Chlebowski, thank you for believing in me through thick and thin.

Misty Stone, I couldn't have survived all the challenges over the years without your invaluable, loving guidance. I love you!

To my friends, Kevin and Monica, thank you for your support and encouragement in the arduous endeavor of writing this book.

To my clients, thank you for believing in the value of my work. You give me the gift of purposeful fulfillment.

To Joshua Lisec, thank you for the motivation and direction to be a published author.

To my mother and father, thank you for having me. I love you.

Divine Source Creator I AM All That Is, thank you for blessing my life and the lives of those who I love. I am humbled by Your loving grace and grateful for the opportunity to be a conduit of Your Light. Thank you.

NATASHA SOL

Author's Bio

Her clients call her "The Real Deal". Because in a turbulent world riddled with spiritual warfare and deception, Natasha Sol is devoted to delivering the purest form of peace, energy, and information. Her delivery is marked with graceful humility, astonishing accuracy, and pristine clarity. Working as a guide to an array of clients including doctors and their patients, actors, solopreneurs, therapists, realtors, contractors, business owners, and law enforcement personnel, Natasha utilizes a unique technique that yields invaluable insight. Her clients often report receiving a soothing sense of clarity and calming resolve, so that they can take steps towards healthy alignment with their inner authority, highest timeline, and most optimal life experience. Learn more at **natashasol.com**.

NATASHA SOL